LEMUR FEELS LET DOWN

A book about DISAPPOINTMENT

Written by Sue Graves

Illustrated by Trevor Dunton

Lemur was **disappointed**. The box of Top Pops was empty! She liked Top Pops for breakfast **every day**. Mum said she could have something else. But Lemur didn't want anything else. She said she wouldn't have any breakfast at all.

That morning, Miss Bird gave the class
a spelling test. Lemur liked spelling tests.
She liked getting them all right. She liked
getting a gold star. But Lemur was **hungry**.

She wished she'd had breakfast. She was so hungry that she couldn't do her spellings. She made **lots of mistakes**. She didn't get a gold star. She felt disappointed.

At playtime, Lemur wanted to play with Tiger. But Tiger was already playing with Hippo. Tiger said he would play with her next, but Lemur got cross. She said she didn't want to play with Tiger anyway!

Lemur ran off. But soon she started to feel lonely.
She wished she'd waited to play with Tiger.

After school, Lemur was going to play with
Cheetah. Cheetah's mum was taking them
to the swamp for a swim.

But Cheetah felt ill. Cheetah's mum said
they would have to go **another day**.
Lemur was disappointed.

Lemur went home. She didn't like feeling disappointed. It made her **feel sad**. She went to find Mum. She told her about all her disappointments. Mum **listened carefully**.

12

13

Lemur's mum said **everyone** felt disappointed
sometimes. She said it was important to deal with
disappointments sensibly. Because Lemur wouldn't
eat **any** breakfast, she couldn't do her spellings.

Because she **wouldn't wait** for Tiger to play,
she ended up having **no one** to play with.
Lemur had a think. She said they weren't sensible
things to do at all!

Then Lemur told Mum about Cheetah. Mum said sometimes it was important to **be patient**. She said it was important to think about **other things** you could do instead.

She said when she was little she wanted to go on the Giant Rocket at the fair. She was **too small**. But she could go on a different ride. It was fun.

The next year she was **big enough** to go on the Giant Rocket. It was brilliant!

Lemur said she could try and be patient.
Mum said that was a very good idea.

Mum said when she felt disappointed, she took
a deep breath and thought about something nice.
Lemur said she could do that, too.

The next day, Lemur ate all her breakfast,
even though there were no Top Pops.

Mum was pleased. Lemur was proud she **hadn't made a fuss.**

At school, Miss Bird gave everyone a spelling test. Lemur tried **really hard**. She was glad that she had eaten her breakfast. She did her spellings carefully. She got them **all right**.

She got a gold star.

At playtime, Lemur wanted to play on the swing. But Monkey was already on it. Lemur felt disappointed.

Then she **remembered** what Mum said. She took a **deep breath**. She played with her other friends instead. She soon forgot about the swing.

After school, Cheetah's mum took Lemur and Cheetah to the swamp. But the swamp had dried up. Cheetah was **disappointed**.

Lemur thought about what they could do instead. She had a good idea. They could make mud pies in the swamp! Cheetah and Lemur said it was the **best day ever**!

A note about sharing this book

The *Behaviour Matters* series has been developed to provide a starting point for further discussion on children's behaviour both in relation to themselves and others. The series is set in the jungle with animal characters reflecting typical behaviour traits often seen in young children.

Lemur Feels Let Down
This story looks at the importance of realising that everyone feels disappointed sometimes, and that learning to compromise and being patient are important skills to develop. It also looks at coping with disappointment in a positive way.

How to use the book
The book is designed for adults to share with either an individual child, or a group of children, and as a starting point for discussion.

The book also provides visual support and repeated words and phrases to build reading confidence.

Before reading the story
Choose a time to read when you and the children are relaxed and have time to share the story.

Spend time looking at the illustrations and talk about what the book might be about before reading it together.

Encourage children to employ a phonics first approach to tackling new words by sounding the words out.

After reading, talk about the book with the children:

- Talk about the story with the children. Encourage them to retell it in their own words.

- Talk about the things that Lemur found disappointing, for example, her favourite cereal not being available; not being able to play with her friends exactly when she wanted to. Invite the children to identify scenarios familiar to their own experiences. Encourage them to talk about situations they find disappointing.

Remind the children to listen quietly and without interruption while others are speaking.

- Ask the children how they deal with feeling disappointed. What do they do to make themselves feel better?

- Place the children into groups and ask them to act out a situation they find disappointing and to include a strategy for how they would overcome their disappointment.

- At the end of the session, select one or two groups to show their performances to the others.

29

For Isabelle, William A, William G, George, Max, Emily,

Leo, Caspar, Felix, Tabitha, Phoebe and Harry –S.G.

Franklin Watts
First published in 2022 by
The Watts Publishing Group

Text © Franklin Watts 2022
Illustrations © Trevor Dunton 2022

The right of Trevor Dunton to be identified as the illustrator
of this Work has been asserted in accordance with the
Copyright, Designs and Patents Act, 1988.

Editor: Jackie Hamley
Designer: Cathryn Gilbert and Peter Scoulding

A CIP catalogue record for this book is available
from the British Library.

ISBN 978 1 4451 7989 6 (hardback)
ISBN 978 1 4451 7990 2 (paperback)
ISBN 978 1 4451 8372 5 (ebook)

Printed in China

Franklin Watts is a division of
Hachette Children's Books,
an Hachette UK company.
www.hachette.co.uk

FSC
www.fsc.org

MIX
Paper from
responsible sources
FSC® C104740